# Mystery on Everest

# Mystery on Everest

## A Photobiography of George Mallory

### By Audrey Salkeld

Foreword by Conrad Anker

NATIONAL GEOGRAPHIC SOCIETY

WASHINGTON, D. C.

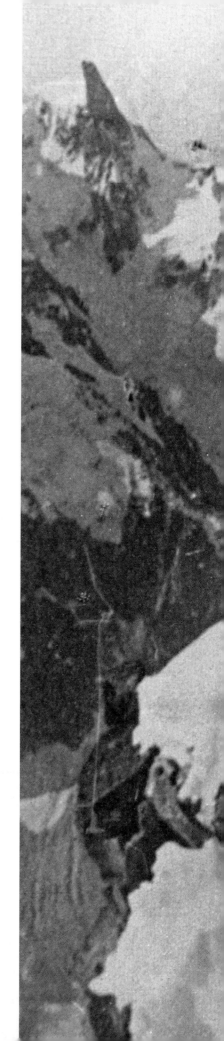

The heroic story of George Mallory and Andrew Irvine has inspired generations of adventure lovers. This book is dedicated to their families who paid so dearly for our inspiration.—AS

**Published by The National Geographic Society**
John M. Fahey, Jr., *President and Chief Executive Officer*
Gilbert M. Grosvenor, *Chairman of the Board*
Nina D. Hoffman, *Senior Vice President*

**Prepared by The Book Division**
William R. Gray, *Vice President and Director*
Charles Kogod, *Assistant Director*
Barbara A. Payne, *Editorial Director and Managing Editor*
David Griffin, *Design Director*

**Staff for this book**
Nancy Laties Feresten, *Director of Children's Publishing*
Suzanne Patrick Fonda, *Editor*
Jennifer Emmett, *Associate Editor and Project Editor*
Marianne Koszorus, *Design Director of Children's Publishing*
David Griffin, *Art Director*
Jo H. Tunstall, *Editorial Assistant*
Meredith Wilcox, *Illustrations Coordinator*
Carl Mehler, *Director of Maps*
Tibor G. Tóth, Michelle H. Picard, Greg Ugiansky, *Map Art and Production*
Anne Marie Houppert, *Indexer*
Lewis R. Bassford, *Production Manager*
Vincent P. Ryan, *Manufacturing Manager*

Library of Congress Cataloging-in-Publication Data
Salkeld, Audrey.
    Mystery on Everest : photobiography of George Mallory / by Audrey Salkeld.
        p. cm.
    Summary: Discusses the life of British mountain climber, George Mallory, the discovery of his body seventy-five years after his death, and the debate over whether Mallory was the first person to reach the top of Mount Everest.
        ISBN 0-7922-7222-6 (hard cover)
    1. Mallory, George Leigh, 1866-1924—Juvenile Literature. 2. Mallory, George Leigh, 1866-1924—Pictorial works—Juvenile Literature. 3. Mountaineers—Great Britain—Biography—Juvenile Literature. 4. Mountaineering—Everest, Mount (China and Nepal)—Juvenile Literature. [1.Mallory, George,1866-1924. 2. Mountaineers. 3. Mountaineering. 4. Everest, Mount (China and Nepal)] 1. Title

GV199.92.L44 S35 2000
769.52'2'092—dc21
[B]                                    00-027645

Printed in the United States of America

**Cover: Mallory's face floats over the ridge on Everest, where he was lost. His ghostly presence haunts the mountain still. Title page: Man of the mountains even when young, George Mallory surveys the Alps. Back cover: 1924 Everest climbing team. Endpapers: The amazing ice pinnacles of the East Rongbuk Glacier.**

*Dear Noel*

*We'll probably start early to-morrow (8th) in order to have clear weather It won't be too early to start looking out for us either crossing the rockband under the pyramid or going up skyline at 8.0 p.m.*

*Yr ever*

*G Mallory*

This is one of the last notes sent down by George Mallory from high on Everest in June 1924. It tells photographer Captain John Noel where to look out for him and Andrew Irvine the next day—"either crossing the rockband under the pyramid or going up skyline." (8.0 p.m. is a mistake; he meant 8.0 a.m.)

# Foreword by Conrad Anker

**G**EORGE LEIGH MALLORY and his drive to climb Mount Everest is an amazing story of determination and ability. The outcome of his final attempt to climb to the highest point on Earth is shrouded in mystery—he and his partner, Andrew Irvine, never returned. They were last seen "moving expeditiously" toward Everest's summit on the 8th of June 1924. An afternoon squall enveloped the mountain, and Noel Odell, their companion who had sighted them, was left to wonder what had happened. Were the two climbers descending from the summit when they vanished? Over the past 75 years mountaineers and historians have pondered the fate of Mallory and Irvine: Could the two climbers have reached the summit of Mount Everest 29 years before Tenzing Norgay and Edmund Hillary in 1953?

The story of George Mallory is about who he was as a person, but it's also about the meaning of exploration. Two important geographic milestones marked the beginning of the 20th century—the conquest of the North Pole in 1909 and the South Pole in 1911. The Third Pole, as Everest was dubbed, was the remaining prize for the exploration community. This goal launched three English expeditions in 1921, 1922 & 1924. The mountain was known to be the highest in the world, yet its formidable flanks had not been surveyed or attempted. A member of all three expeditions, Mallory was the person who defined Everest climbing. In 1921 his expert mountain sense opened the route on the north side, which is still climbed today. By 1922 the climbers knew the route, the timing of the monsoon, and the demands altitude places on the body. Mallory returned for this third attempt in the spring of 1924.

Seventy-five years later, on the first of May 1999, while climbing Everest, my teammates and I discovered the body of George Mallory.

Mallory's nailed boot was found on Everest in 1999. Climbers in those days selected the pattern of bootnails they felt would best safeguard their footing on different types of ground.

The new information yielded from artifacts and the placement of the body shed light on the difficulties Mallory and Irvine faced on their last day. They were exhausted, dehydrated, and the climbing was hard. It is likely the storm forced them to turn back before reaching the summit.

Regardless of whether Mallory and Irvine summitted Everest in 1924, their story is one of great interest. They were trying something that had never been done before, and their task was daunting. How did humans function at extreme altitude? Was their equipment adequate? Would there be bad weather? Mallory and Irvine applied organization, experience, and determination in answering these questions. Their efforts are an inspiration. Mountain climbing doesn't produce material goods nor does it provide a service. Mountains are representations of goals in our lives. Your dreams may be in the mountains or the world around you; they are worth striving for.

"Because it's there," Mallory's famous reply when asked why he choose to climb Mount Everest, is as timely today as it was then. These simple and thoughtful words give us the courage to try something unknown, to better ourselves, and to persevere.

# Growing Up

## "Life is like a dream."

GEORGE LEIGH MALLORY WAS BORN into a comfortable family in rural England on June 18, 1886. His father, Herbert Leigh Mallory, was a clergyman in the village of Mobberley, a parish he had taken over from his own father. He fervently hoped young George would in time also become a minister.

George was second of the four lively children of Herbert and his wife, Annie. Like his two sisters and his younger brother, he loved the Mobberley countryside, with its thickets of trees and a brook. His sense of adventure showed itself early.

At the age of seven—so one story goes—after being sent to his room for bad behavior, George was spotted climbing on the nearby church roof. "But I *did* go to my room," he protested when scolded, "to fetch my cap."

His sister Avie (short for Annie Victoria) remembered, "It was always such fun doing things with George. He had the knack of making things exciting and often rather dangerous. I learnt very early that it was fatal to tell him that any tree was impossible for him to get up. 'Impossible' was a word that acted as a challenge to him." When George told her that it ought to be possible to lie between the railway lines and let a train run over him, Avie kept as quiet as a mouse for fear he would really try to do it.

The young Mallorys were sent away to school at the age of 10 or 11.

As a small boy George, at center, climbed everything it was possible to climb. His sense of adventure was inherited from his mother, Annie. His sisters, Avie (left) and Mary (right), adored him.

W. W. Winter.

THE ALEXANDRA ROOMS
DERBY.

George picnics with his sister Mary (above). He demonstrates good balance (right) as the centerpiece of a gymnastics display at Winchester College. He shone at gymnastics and was the only boy in school to master the bold "giant swing" on the horizontal bar.

George didn't mind: He saw it as an adventure to be away from home. Geometry was his favorite subject, and he won a mathematics scholarship to high school at Winchester College, Britain's oldest school. It was during his final years at Winchester that George was introduced to mountaineering by his housemaster, Graham Irving. Irving invited George and his friend Harry Gibson to spend a summer holiday in the Alps. Although George and Harry began the trip with severe headaches from altitude sickness, they quickly recovered. The trip was in every other way a success, and George fell in love with climbing mountains.

AT COLLEGE AT CAMBRIDGE UNIVERSITY, Mallory studied history. He wasn't sure what he wanted to do with his life beyond making the world a better place. He considered following family tradition and going into the church

but eventually swung around to the idea of becoming a teacher. As a teacher, he could shape young minds, champion the "right" of things, and believe in God and Good, while leaving theology, or religious theory, for others to wrestle with.

When he was in college, Mallory escaped whenever he could to climb in the British hills. Once, when he was climbing in Wales, he realized he had left his pipe on a ledge halfway down one of the regular routes. He took a shortcut to retrieve it before scrambling back the same way. Nobody saw the exact line he followed, but when other climbers took a look the next day, they saw a rock overhanging so far that it was hard to

At Cambridge University, George studied history, but he also enjoyed literature, drama, politics, and debate. He was captain of Magdalene College Boat Club (left, without cap). In his final year he decided to become a teacher rather than a clergyman like his father.

*"To see the Alps Again! How glorious it will be, after dreaming of them for four years!"*

imagine how he could have climbed it at all. The route was officially recorded by the Climbers' Club as Mallory's Pipe, with the description: "This climb is totally impossible. It has been performed once, in failing light, by Mr. G.H.L. Mallory."

Early in 1909, Mallory was introduced to the famous mountaineer Geoffrey Winthrop Young, who would become a lifelong friend and mentor. Ten years his senior, with a fine record of new Alpine ascents, Young was known for his long days in the mountains. A midnight or 1 a.m. start was nothing out of the ordinary for him, and he could keep going for 20 hours or more. When Young suggested Mallory climb with him in the Alps that summer, he needed little persuading.

They were joined in Switzerland by Donald Robertson, another of Young's friends, and decided to first climb the Nesthorn, by way of a long ridge. This became the site of one of Mallory's closest calls.

By late afternoon they'd reached the last dark tower on the ridge. Mallory was in the lead. He traversed, or moved across, out onto the scoop of the mountain's south face, before beginning to wrestle his way upward. And then, when he was attempting a gymnastic swing up the overhanging wall, it happened. Young saw the boots "flash from the wall without even a scrape," and an equally soundless gray streak flickered past him and out of sight below. Mallory fell 40 feet without touching rock. Young flung himself forward onto the belay that anchored him to the cliff, grinding the rope and his hands into the slab of rock before him, to stop Mallory's fall. Miraculously, though vibrating like an elastic band, the hemp rope held.

Mallory, dangling above the glacier, was unhurt and unflustered and had not even lost hold of his ice ax. "Let out more rope, and lower away," he called, and soon climbed back up to rejoin Young. The whole

George Mallory lounges in North Wales (above) with the talented climber Siegfried Herford at left. This picture was taken at Christmas 1913 after the pair had made a new rock climb on Lliwedd, the "Double Girdle Traverse," with Geoffrey Young. As a teacher, Mallory (below, left) often introduced his students to mountain climbing over school vacations.

# "She's good as gold and brave and true and sweet. What more can I say?"

thing was over so quickly that Robertson, some way below them and around a corner, had no idea anything had taken place at all.

WHEN MALLORY BEGAN TEACHING at Charterhouse, a boys' school in Surrey, in September 1910, he arrived full of ideas and theories. One student has told how he and his friends regarded their idealistic young schoolmaster: "He was pale and, to our unskilled eyes, weedy, far from athletic. He taught English and really seemed to enjoy poetry, even when he had to listen to our faltering repetition of standard passages. Discipline, he had no idea of keeping. On one occasion he was put on the floor and we sat on his head."

During his third year at Charterhouse, George Mallory met the three Turner sisters, Marjorie, Ruth, and Mildred. Their mother had died seven years before, and they lived across the river from the school with their architect father in a grand house he had built on a hill to the west of town. George became a regular visitor, and soon he and the middle daughter, Ruth, were engaged.

George's father performed the ceremony, and guests commented that the happy couple looked almost too good to be true. For their honeymoon, George had wanted to take Ruth climbing in the Alps, but within days of the wedding World War I broke out. So, instead of seeing Switzerland, the bridal pair went walking in Devon and Sussex. One night they slept out on a beach—and were arrested, briefly, on suspicion of being German spies!

George married Ruth Turner in the summer of 1914 within a week of the outbreak of World War I. In 1916, George said good-bye to Ruth and their new baby and crossed to France to fight.

During the war Mallory was posted to the front lines in charge of heavy howitzers, or guns, with the task of pounding German positions. He liked it best when he was sent forward to man one of the observation posts.

As young men flocked to France to fight, Mallory stayed at home. Teaching was a protected occupation, which meant he could not join the army without his headmaster's permission. For a while, settling into a new house and with Ruth expecting their first baby, who would be named Clare, he was happy. But as time passed, and his friends and even former students began dying in battle, he became restless and depressed. Mallory felt he should be with them. But his headmaster refused to let him go. Finally, a replacement was found for him and he was released to begin training as a second lieutenant in the Royal Garrison Artillery. He crossed to France on May 4, 1916.

The campaigning side of army life, which involved a lot of "roughing it," living under canvas or in trenches, and being constantly on the move, held no terrors for Mallory. Physical discomfort had never bothered him; even as a boy he'd made a habit of sometimes sleeping without blankets so he could get used to being cold.

Of course there were harsher realities and times when Mallory and his comrades came under heavy fire. He was relieved to find that he did not faint at the sight of blood or bodies. "But, oh! The pity of it!" he wrote. "Like cutting off buds." When he had a narrow escape from a bullet, he wrote Ruth that he was more worried for her than for himself. "But," he reminded her, "we settled long ago that there's no reckoning with Death."

After a year he was sent home to England for an operation on an old ankle injury and was able to spend precious time with Ruth before their second daughter, Beridge, was born in September. This was when news came that his climbing friend Geoffrey Young had been badly wounded in battle. His left leg had to be amputated above the knee. Mallory was appalled. "It's the spoiling of some flawless, perfect thing," he told Geoffrey's mother. "We had promised each other days on the mountains together...and I can't separate my own loss in it from his."

A whole year passed before Mallory finally got back to France for the last of the war, by which time there was little to do but keep himself and his men amused. He organized sports days and ran classes for the troops, besides setting aside time each day for his own reading and writing.

Like everyone, Mallory was impatient to get home once the armistice, the truce ending the fighting, was signed that November, but it was spring of 1919 before he and Ruth were reunited.

They moved back into their home, "The Holt"—which they had rented to friends during the war—and Mallory returned to his teaching job at Charterhouse. The house was perfect for them—"swarming with boys" as a climbing colleague, Cottie Sanders, observed. But though he seemed happy, Mallory was restless.

He was ready for a new challenge.

# Everest

## "Because it's there."

FOR MOST OF MAN'S HISTORY no one knew which was the highest mountain on Earth. Then, surveyors in the Himalaya in the 19th century realized that here were peaks taller than any others. A popular story tells how one day in 1852 the Bengali chief computer of the Survey of India—a man, that was, not a machine!—rushed into his boss's office shouting, "Sir! Sir! I've discovered the highest mountain in the world."

It was an unnamed mountain on the border between Tibet and Nepal, identified merely by its survey number "Peak 15." It was reckoned to be 29,002 feet.

Clearly, such an important mountain needed a name rather than a number. It was survey policy to use local names wherever possible, but so far inquiries had not turned up any. So "Mount Everest" was suggested, in commemoration of Sir George Everest, an earlier surveyor general.

Once Everest was recognized as the world's tallest mountain, it was natural to wonder if humans would ever reach its summit.

The early Everest expeditions were organized in the 1920s by the Royal Geographical Society and the Alpine Club in London, and George Mallory was invited to join. At first he wasn't sure he could leave Ruth and the children, but in the end both George and Ruth decided it was too good an opportunity to miss.

The job of the first expedition in 1921 was to find the best way to reach the mountain through unknown Tibet, and to

Members of the 1921 Everest Reconnaissance Expedition. Back row, left to right: Sandy Wollaston, Charles Howard-Bury, A.M. Heron, and Harold Raeburn. Front row: George Mallory, E.O. Wheeler, Guy Bullock and H.T. Morshead. (Opposite) A sketch of Mallory, drawn by Colonel Edward Norton in 1924.

identify, if possible, a route to the summit. An actual climbing attempt would only be made if time permitted.

Though he was excited about going, Mallory was worried that most of the team were rather elderly and more mountain travelers than climbers. A few weeks before departure, George Ingle Finch, the one other young climber in the group, failed his medical exam. Mallory quickly suggested an old friend from Winchester, Guy Bullock, as a replacement. To his relief, Bullock was promptly welcomed onto the team.

The members met up in Darjeeling, India, from where they set off in two parties in the middle of May 1921 with their trains of porters, cooks,

and mules. They were a raggle-taggle crew dressed in old tweeds, military raincoats, and hand-knitted woollen scarves and socks very different from the polar fleece and Gore-Tex of modern climbers. The route took them first through the tea gardens and steamy forests of Sikkim, then over the Himalayan crest to the barren tableland of Tibet with its strong, chill winds. Crossing this in a great arc, they planned to approach Everest from the north. Then the expedition's first calamity struck.

A messenger panted up to say that Dr. Alexander Kellas, the team's foremost Himalaya expert, had died coming over the last pass. He had not been well for days and was being carried on a stretcher when his heart suddenly gave out. This was a terrible blow. The team buried him on a stony hillside overlooking the plain, with three great snow peaks in the distance that he alone had climbed.

This map opposite shows the South Asia as it was in the 1920s, when the English first attempted to climb Mount Everest. Mallory wanted to call the beautiful snow peak above "Clare" after his first-born daughter (left), but was told firmly that personal names would not be "allowed to stick." A local-sounding name had to be invented, and the mountain became "Pumori," which translates as "Honorable Daughter."

Just visible on the horizon, a hundred miles away, was the mountain they had all come to see—Everest.

They continued through Shegar Dzong, the regional capital, and set up expedition headquarters in Tingri village, a few days' walk from Everest. Mallory and Bullock headed for the long wind-scoured valley of the Rongbuk below Everest's north face to look for a good route to the summit. They took with them sixteen of the best porters and the team's interpreter, Gyalzen. They pitched their tents at 16,500 feet, close to the Rongbuk Monastery and not far from where modern-day Everest expeditions have their base camps. Then they tirelessly tramped the glaciers and the moraines (the piles of debris that the glaciers deposited), and scrambled up to passes and subsidiary peaks, surveying, photographing, looking for the best way up the mountain.

"We're just about to walk off the map....
It's beginning to be exciting."

Ice formations on the Central Rongbuk Glacier march from the foot of Mount
Everest. This photograph was taken by Mallory in 1921 from a nearby peak.

*"...it has the most steep ridges and appalling precipices that I have ever seen, and...all the talk of an easy snow slope is a myth."*

For almost a month Mallory and Bullock covered a phenomenal amount of ground, scouting out the mountain's northern side. The only valley they didn't investigate was one from which a small side stream emerged to run under the Main Rongbuk Glacier. This proved a mistake. It would have proved the easiest approach but was discovered too late to be of use to that year's expedition.

Instead, on August 18, they struggled in the thin air to the crest of a pass in mountains to the east, which they called Windy Gap. There, ahead, lay the East Rongbuk Glacier, giving access to the slopes of Everest. Mallory was overjoyed. He wrote proudly to Ruth of "a supreme effort made and happily rewarded; of a big task accomplished." He fairly puffed out his chest with pride, he told her, adding, "How we wished it had been possible to follow it down and find out the secret of its exit." But there was no time for backtracking. If they were to get to grips with Everest's slopes this season, they had to go forward, across Windy Gap.

On the last day of August, Mallory and Bullock made it to 20,000 feet, where they camped on a stony ledge above the Kharta Glacier. Bad weather pinned them in their tents for the first two weeks of September. Mallory, after a bout of tonsillitis, was losing strength, but at last, on September 17, he and his party were able to set off once more with their strongest porters and 11 loads.

Two days later all the climbers except Harold Raeburn made it to Windy Gap at 22,350 feet, where, tucked under the rim for shelter, they spent a very cold and cheerless night.

(Opposite) George Mallory, ice ax in hand, trains Sherpa porters in ice-climbing techniques. Although the 1921 expedition was meant only to be a scouting mission, Mallory hoped for an attempt on the summit.

An hour or so after sunrise, Mallory, Bullock, and Wheeler set off to cross the snow basin with their three strongest porters and began plodding up the steep, heavily snow-laden slopes of the North Col, a saddle-shaped depression in the mountain. "Nothing very remarkable remains in my mind about the ascent," Mallory reported later, "except perhaps Wheeler's black beard coming up behind me." By 11:30 a.m. they had reached the top of the col, where a gale was blowing to snatch their breath away.

Mallory was sure that had they been fresher, or the wind less violent, this route could have led them to the summit. As it was, to push on would be madness. No man, he told Ruth, could live in that wind for more than an hour. They attempted a few more steps to put the matter to the test, then quickly scuttled back below the lip of the col.

The expedition was over.

Throughout the long sea voyage home, Mallory could not shake off a sense of failure. He kept to his cabin for the most part, writing furiously. He missed Ruth and the children and was homesick for London and the English countryside.

He had been away for seven months—and for what? Repeatedly, he went over the attempt in his memory. By the time they were steaming toward Marseilles, France, where Ruth had traveled to meet him, he felt easier in his mind. Now he could only feel relief that he hadn't been tempted to go farther with such pitifully inadequate resources.

This panoramic photograph (top) shows the little camp from where Mallory and his companions approached and climbed the North Col of Everest, right. Roped for safety, the reconnaissance team descends in monsoon snows (bottom).

# Second Attempt

*"...There is something in man which responds to the challenge of this mountain and goes out to meet it..."*

ONE LESSON LEARNED was that the best time to launch an attempt on the summit would be in the short settled period before the monsoon season, which brought heavy snow. This meant arriving in base camp during April or early May, rather than in June. Mallory spent only three months at home before sailing east to take up the struggle once more.

George Ingle Finch, who had failed the medical exam the previous year, passed in 1922. As a scientist, he would be in charge of the oxygen equipment that was being sent out to help the climbers breathe in the low-oxygen air of the mountain. It would be the first time that oxygen equipment had ever been used for mountain climbing, and it was not popular. Mallory couldn't bear the idea of working with a rubber mask over his face—"I sicken at the thought of the saliva dribbling down," he told Ruth. Even though he knew it made him tire quickly, he was perfectly content to work with the limited amount of oxygen available in God's fresh air.

All in all, this was a happy and friendly party, thanks to the leadership of the popular General Charlie Bruce. Mallory and Henry Morshead were the only two climbers to have been on the earlier expedition, but several of the porters were old hands. Newcomers included Major Edward "Teddy" Norton, a great sportsman and naturalist, T. Howard Somervell and Arthur Wakefield, both doctors from the English Lake District, and six others, including Captain John Noel, the official photographer.

This time, the team made straight for the East Rongbuk Glacier,

Members of the 1922 expedition gaze in awe at the Himalayan chain. Everest is on the left, and to the right are the peaks of Gyachung-Kang and Cho Oyu.

which had yet to be explored along its whole 12-mile length. Bruce marched them, burly and fit, into the Rongbuk Valley on the last day of April. On the first of May they set up Base Camp within a mile of the snout of the Rongbuk Glacier. That night the team drank Bruce's health in champagne.

Four team members set off to explore the glacier and settle on the campsites. Cooks were installed in all camps, and throughout the month supplies, equipment, and oxygen bottles continued to move "up the line." Mallory and Somervell climbed the dangerous slopes of the col to erect the first tents ever on an icy shelf just below its crest.

Almost everyone had been suffering some degree of stomach illness, brought on by altitude. Finch had been hit worst and was stuck in bed

The 1922 expedition group photograph (top) shows the climbing team supported by their porters and Gurkha assistants. The leader, General Bruce, sits fifth from the left, front row, with Mallory standing behind him. General Bruce presides at the head of the table (bottom).

for several days. The original plan was for two summit bids: the first by Mallory and Somervell without oxygen, to be followed a day or so later by Finch and Norton climbing with oxygen bottles. But with Finch sick, and with fears that the monsoon could soon be upon them, there was an abrupt change. Finch was horrified, on looking out of his tent, to see the four fittest climbers setting off together. Where did that leave him? Was oxygen to be given no trial at all? His spirits crashed.

Climbing with nine porters, Mallory, Somervell, Norton, and Morshead mounted the North Col, pitched more tents, and slept there. Early the next morning they would set off up the spine of the North Ridge, taking the first footsteps on the true slopes of the mountain, where endurance and the will to go on would determine all.

Mallory was up at five o'clock to rouse the others but discovered that half the porters were suffering from altitude sickness and could climb no higher. Plus, breakfast was frozen solid. It was seven o'clock before they got under way. A cold wind buffeted them from the west.

Without crampons (detachable metal frames with spikes) on their boots, they had to cut steps in the steep snow to safeguard their feet. By midday they were all glad to halt in the shelter of some rocks at about 25,000 feet. This was not where they hoped to set up their Camp 5, but they couldn't go higher. They built two small platforms of stacked stones and erected their little tents. The porters, freezing without wind-proof clothing, were sent hurrying back to the col.

(Opposite) Mallory, left, and Norton approach their high point of 26,985 feet
on the North Ridge. The drawing above was prepared for Captain Noel's film
of the 1922 expedition. It shows the approach to Everest, the campsites, and
the record heights achieved by the two climbing groups.

In the night the wind dropped, but as dawn approached Mallory was
disgusted to hear fine hail pattering on the tents. Again, there would be
no early start. When, at eight o'clock, they were ready to set off,
Morshead, who had caught cold the day before, announced that he'd
stay behind so he wouldn't keep them back. Disappointed, the others
pressed on without him. A thin layer of snow covered the sloping
footholds and slowed progress. Hugging the ridge, they made for the
Northeast Shoulder. Progress was painfully slow. By 2 p.m. it was clear
they would not reach the shoulder and get back in time to bring
Morshead to the North Col. They turned back.

Their trail had been destroyed, and the ground was slippery. They
roped themselves together and cut steps as they descended. Morshead,

*"It's all on the knees of the gods, and they are bare cold knees."*

when they collected him, was shaky on his feet. At one point he skidded out of the steps Mallory had cut for him and could not stop himself. Norton and Somervell were caught off guard. Before anyone realized, they too were tugged off their feet and falling.

Luckily Mallory was alert. He heard a noise, rammed in his ice ax, and wrapped their safety rope around it. With supreme strength he held his ground and stopped the other three.

Badly shaken, they continued their nightmare descent. It was long after dark by the time they picked their way around the crevasses on the North Col, supporting Morshead, and 11:30 p.m. before they got back to their tents. They found the porters had taken away all the cooking pots, leaving them no way of melting snow for a drink. They had to mix jam and canned milk to quench their raging thirst. They all knew they were lucky to be alive.

Finch, meanwhile, had been working to improve his situation. If there were no climbers to accompany him on his oxygen attempt, then he must train a couple of recruits: Geoffrey Bruce, the transport officer, and Lance-Corporal Tejbir, an Indian army officer. They spent three days preparing the oxygen apparatus and gathering porters together. As the four exhausted members of the first party made their way down to Camp 3, Finch and his retinue climbed past them to the col on a training exercise. Two days later they were ready to make their climb.

Finch and his team moved Camp 5 some 500 feet higher up the North Ridge, still short of the 26,000 feet he had hoped for. Tucking themselves into Camp 5, they sent the porters back down. Fierce winds threatened to blow away their tents and kept them in camp the next day and night. Before daybreak on the 27th they began thawing their boots over a candle, and as the first rays of sun caught the tent, they were off.

Finch and Bruce return from their record climb with oxygen (left). Finch, behind, is wearing the down-filled coat he designed to keep warm on Everest. Above, Finch demonstrates the expedition's oxygen apparatus. Loaded with four bottles, it weighed over 30 pounds and was used to make breathing easier. In effect, the air at Everest's summit has one third the oxygen of the air at sea level.

Tejbir, lacking windproof clothing, soon began to tire and was sent back to wait in the tent. Finch and Bruce struck out across the slabby ledges of the North Face, climbing unroped for speed. It was tricky underfoot, with layers of snow and pebbles. When they stopped to change empty oxygen cylinders, they sent them clanging down the mountainside shouting, "Another five pounds off our backs!"

Their horizontal progress was good, and Finch gradually changed tack to gain height as well. Soon, their barometer was reading 27,300 feet, and they could see they were higher than all the other peaks around. Then Bruce let out a startled cry. His oxygen had ceased flowing, and he began to stumble. Finch moved swiftly. Grabbing Bruce's shoulder and steering him to a ledge, he passed over his own oxygen mask while he worked to fix Bruce's equipment. Despite the brain-numbing altitude, Finch managed to make the repair, but he could see, looking up at the summit, that there was no way they could climb that far in their exhausted state. If they pressed on, it was almost certain one or both of them would never come back.

Back in Base Camp, the climbers took stock, and despite their frost-bitten and exhausted state, Mallory decided they should try for one more attempt. So, on June 7 he led 14 laden porters up into the North Col, which was heavy with newly fallen snow.

There were four ropes of men, with all the Europeans on the first rope, scouting the way. They had climbed about 100 feet when Mallory

heard something like an explosion. A small slab of snow had broken away to the right of the party and was sliding toward them. Those on his rope were only lightly covered and quickly climbed out. Those in the group behind were picked up and dropped 100 feet lower. Of the remaining nine men, there was no sign. They had been carried over an ice cliff into a crevasse and buried under many feet of avalanched snow. The fall alone would have killed most.

Despite frantic digging, only two men were recovered from the crevasse. Altogether, seven men died, the last in the column, and all of them porters. Mallory was devastated and held himself largely responsible. Once more, he returned from Everest bitter and depressed. And once more the Everest Committee faced the prospect of organizing a return expedition.

Camp on the North Col (left) was a cold and windy spot. Frostbitten and exhausted after his high climb, Geoffrey Bruce is assisted down the East Rongbuk Glacier (right).

"Do you know that sickening feeling that one can't go back and have it undone and that nothing will make good?"

From Camp 3 members watched Mallory and Somervell lead a column of climbers up the snow-heavy slopes of the North Col. Minutes later, the column had vanished, carried away in an avalanche. When the dust settled, some figures could be seen struggling free, but seven porters had died.

# Last Climb

*"For the stone from the top for geologists, the knowledge of the limits of endurance for the doctors, but above all for the spirit of adventure to keep alive the soul of man."*

EXPERIENCE HAD TAUGHT some lessons. First, of course, that even gentle slopes should be avoided after fresh snowfall. Camp 5 should be placed as high as possible. And, ideally, placing a Camp 6 at about 27,000 feet would reduce the distance facing climbers on summit day. The performance of the high-altitude porters had been tremendous, and there was every reason to suppose they might be persuaded to carry supplies to an even higher camp.

It was harder to evaluate the value of the bottled oxygen. Those climbing without it had managed to adapt to the altitude fairly well. Though everyone struggled whenever a new elevation was reached, the discomfort eased each time they climbed down and back again. And although Finch and Bruce climbed 215 vertical feet higher and a mile farther horizontally than Mallory's oxygenless party, there was nothing to suggest they came down much fitter or fresher than those who had not used it. It seemed that, given favorable conditions, a man could reach the summit of the highest mountain, whether he climbed with oxygen or without it

So—should they or shouldn't they equip a fresh expedition with the controversial apparatus? It was costly and unpredictable in its performance, and it devoured porter effort. And if they took it, should they all use it, or only those who wanted to? This was never resolved. A hastily

George Mallory and Andrew "Sandy" Irvine are shown onboard ship heading to Everest in 1924. Mallory encouraged the less experienced Irvine. "Just the sort of person to depend upon for anything," he said, "except perhaps conversation."

redesigned version was sent out with the next party. Mallory was persuaded of its usefulness, but it remained unpopular with most of the climbers.

Mallory and Finch embarked on a series of lectures to raise money for a new expedition and to satisfy the enormous public curiosity about the climb. Mallory returned from a speaking tour in America in early 1923, and landed a post in Cambridge teaching working-class men and women. He threw himself into his new life and pushed Everest from his mind. But not for long.

In 1924 the British set out again to conquer Everest. The core of the team remained the same: Mallory, Norton, Somervell, Geoffrey Bruce, and Noel, but there was new blood too. One of the newcomers was Andrew Irvine, an engineering student at Oxford. Though he could boast little climbing experience, he was strong, resourceful, and cheerful, an ideal companion on a rugged venture. At 21, he was younger than the committee had in mind, but his reputation for being a mechanical genius tipped the balance in his favor.

General Bruce started out as team leader once again, but when the team reached Tibet he came down with an alarming case of malaria and had to be escorted back down. Norton took charge and appointed Mallory "climbing leader." Throughout the rest of the trek, these two discussed their assault plan endlessly. They hoped to put two teams of two climbers—one with and one without oxygen—on top by May 17.

Unfortunately, on reaching Rongbuk, they were greeted by a biting wind and winter snow still on the ground. Nevertheless, they began setting up camps and ferrying loads up the East Rongbuk Glacier. They would have been better off waiting.

Mallory and Irvine led a protesting band of porters through blizzards to the site of Camp 3 under the North Col. Everyone suffered badly from the altitude, and not having managed to carry up enough food, stoves, or bedding, they faced a viciously cold night on the ice. Next morning many were sick and vomiting. Mallory raced up and down between camps trying to get men and loads into the right place, but everyone was miserable and exhausted.

At Base Camp, the 1924 team. Irvine and Mallory are standing at left. Beside them: Norton, Noel Odell, and John Macdonald (*The Times* messenger). Seated, left to right: E.O. Shebbeare, Geoffrey Bruce, Somervell, and Bentley Beetham.

When Norton and Geoffrey Bruce followed a day or two later, there was some restoration of spirits, but no improvement in the weather. By May 11, they still had not scaled the North Col, and precious fuel was being burned with nothing to show for it. Norton called everyone off the mountain.

Several of the porters were frostbitten, one so seriously it was clear he would lose both feet. Another fell during the descent and broke his leg. Worst of all, one of the Indian army helpers lay unconscious in Camp 1 with a suspected blood clot on the brain. This man died shortly afterward while being carried down to Base Camp. Later, the man with

the hideous frostbite also succumbed. Both were buried across the river from Base Camp.

The team gathered in Camp 1 for a council of war. Norton favored forgetting about oxygen and concentrating porter power in getting the two high camps set up and supplied. Two pairs of climbers could then make dashes at the summit if conditions allowed. To Mallory's mind this was throwing away any chance of success. With time at a premium, he was now convinced that oxygen alone held the key. But he had to accept Norton's decision.

So, on June 1, Mallory and Geoffrey Bruce moved up the North Ridge to establish Camp 5. Half of their porters dumped loads 300 feet short of the proposed campsite, leaving Bruce and the fittest of the others to ferry them up while Mallory did his best to level out two platforms for the tents. They all spent an uncomfortable night on the steep slope, and

The East Rongbuk Glacier (left) was a fairyland on a good day, but it could be hell on Earth when blizzards raged. To make the ascent of the North Col easier for laden porters, young Irvine constructed a long rope ladder (right).

in the morning the remaining porters refused to go on. Mallory sent them down with a note for Norton. "Show's crashed," it said.

Before long, he and Bruce followed. Once again, reality had fallen short of Mallory's imagining. He could not see how the second party of Norton and Somervell, veterans from the 1922 attempt, already on their way up to 5, would do much better if they too were without oxygen. Tired as he was, he began planning one last attempt with oxygen. Everything rested on him now, he believed.

The weather held fine for Norton and Somervell, who were able to set up Camp 6, a single tent, in a rocky little basin at 26,700 feet on the North Face. They had little appetite and made do with coffee and soup that evening. At 6:45 a.m., they started out. Norton chipped his way across the snowy patches until they reached the distinctive band of yellow limestone that encircles the mountain. This had weathered into horizontal ledges, which proved easier to climb than the tilted, gravel-coated slabs were.

Porter Namgya (above) suffered frostbitten fingers from the cold; he later recovered fully. Colonel Norton (right) makes his lonely way across the North Face of Everest to reach a record height of 28,126 feet, but the summit remained elusive.

The altitude was beginning to bother them. Every few yards the men bent over their ice axes, gasping for breath. At about 28,000 feet, Somervell, who had an agonizing sore throat, felt too weak to continue. He urged Norton to go on without him. It was a fine, bright day, though very cold. Norton had made the mistake of taking off his goggles to see more clearly and was experiencing the first signs of snow blindness. But he reached the gash on the North Face that is now known as Norton's Couloir and picked his way gingerly across it.

Beyond, the going got steeper. It was like climbing on roof tiles, Norton said, too dangerous for a single, unroped climber. One slip could pitch him into the void. Though the summit pyramid looked tantalizingly close, only another 200 vertical feet above, he knew it was beyond him. Turning around, he clambered back to rejoin Somervell. His high point was later calculated as 28,126 feet.

At Camp 6 they stopped only long enough to pack knapsacks and continued down toward the col. But progress was extraordinarily slow. Somervell nearly choked to death on the way when the lining of his frozen throat peeled away and stuck in his windpipe. He sank into the snow to die, but with one last heave of his chest, he was able to clear the obstruction and breathe freely. By the time they reached the tents of Camp 6, Norton was completely blind.

"It's fifty to one against us but we'll have a whack yet and do ourselves proud."

A photograph by Somervell shows the view from 28,000 feet.

Mallory had been fiercely busy while the pair were away. Determined that he and Irvine should make a third attempt if Somervell and Norton failed, they had been to Camp 3 to round up fit porters, whatever stores they needed, and—most important—all available oxygen cylinders. As Norton lay sightless in his tent on the col, Mallory outlined his plans.

Norton would have preferred Mallory to make the attempt with Noel Odell, their geologist, who seemed much fitter and had far more mountaineering experience, but young Irvine was eager and certainly was the best at keeping the temperamental oxygen equipment in shape. He had been working on it throughout the expedition, improving all the loose connections and streamlining its design. Norton could understand why Mallory wanted to climb with Irvine. He had taken him under his wing from the start, and the pair were now firm friends who worked well together. The leader knew better than to challenge Mallory's decision and wished them well.

On the morning of Friday, June 6, Odell got up early to fry some sardines for the departing climbers. It was a kind gesture, if not particularly appetizing. He was sorry they ate so little, but they were anxious to be off. Odell took their picture as they were about to leave, with their oxygen frames on their backs. It was the last picture taken of them alive.

With them went eight porters, climbing without oxygen but carrying all the available spare cylinders. That evening four of the porters returned with a note to Norton saying there was remarkably little wind up there and that "things look hopeful."

The remaining four stayed with Mallory and Irvine throughout the next morning as they continued to Camp 6. Then they, too, came down bearing notes from Mallory. One was for Odell, but the other note was for the photographer, Captain Noel, advising him where to watch for them next day. "It won't be too early to start looking out for us either crossing the rockband under the pyramid or going up skyline at 8.0 p.m.," Mallory wrote. Presumably he intended to write 8.0 a.m., and we suppose that when he said he'd make an early start he meant something between 5 and 6 a.m., when it would first get light. So Mallory thought he could get from camp to the pyramid just below the summit

The last photograph of Mallory and Irvine alive (above) shows them preparing to leave the North Col Camp on June 6. They died two days later. Some of Mallory's belongings (left) were recovered when his body was discovered 75 years later. His goggles, penknife, and altimeter—missing its indicator hand—were found in his pockets.

in about three hours. Now that modern climbers have taken that route to Everest, we know that Mallory was wrong. Modern climbers would start their summit day very soon after midnight, and from a camp closer to the top.

Next day, however, when Odell was climbing up to Camp 6, he looked up at 12:50 p.m. and saw two dots on the ridge. One dot, he was convinced, moved to join the other on a small snow crest before the vision was lost in cloud. Mallory and Irvine! What alarmed him was that, although they seemed to be moving "with considerable alacrity," they were very late according his understanding of Mallory's proposed schedule. Had they met with unforeseen difficulties, or was the oxygen equipment acting up?

Unfortunately, Odell was never quite clear about the exact position of his sighting. At first he said that his friends were "on ridge, nearing base of final pyramid"; later he would place them on top of the second of the two rock steps. When doubts were expressed about whether anyone—even George Mallory—could climb this major feature in as few minutes as he described, Odell agreed that the pair may have been only at the first step. Even though he was never able to pinpoint the spot, throughout his long life Odell steadfastly maintained that he had seen Mallory and Irvine that day. Not everyone believed him.

When Odell reached Camp 6 about an hour later, a snow squall was blowing up, and he was happy to duck inside the little tent. The chaos of strewn belongings and oxygen bits and pieces that greeted him reinforced his belief that there must have been a last-minute problem with the oxygen. After a while he decided to climb higher in case his friends were trying to find their way back in the storm. He yodeled and whistled, but his voice was lost in the wind. At times he was forced to shelter from the sleety blasts behind rocks. There was no trace of Mallory and Irvine, and he went back to the tent just as the storm blew over and the mountain was bathed in sunshine. Again he scanned the upper crags but saw nothing.

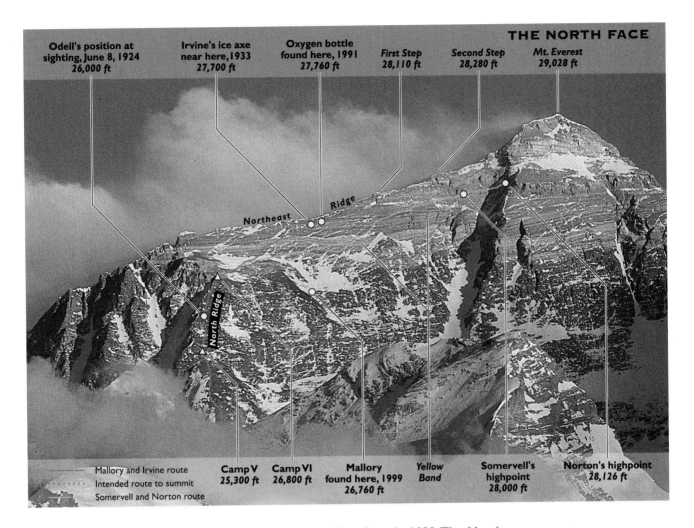

**Odell's position at sighting, June 8, 1924** 26,000 ft

**Irvine's ice axe near here, 1933** 27,700 ft

**Oxygen bottle found here, 1991** 27,760 ft

**First Step** 28,110 ft

**Second Step** 28,280 ft

**Mt. Everest** 29,028 ft

Northeast Ridge

North Ridge

Mallory and Irvine route
Intended route to summit
Somervell and Norton route

**Camp V** 25,300 ft

**Camp VI** 26,800 ft

**Mallory found here, 1999** 26,760 ft

**Yellow Band**

**Somervell's highpoint** 28,000 ft

**Norton's highpoint** 28,126 ft

Irvine's ice ax (opposite) was discovered below the First Step in 1933. The North Face of Everest (above) shows the route and camps of the 1924 expedition and the position of some of the finds relating to Mallory and Irvine's accident.

Mallory had warned Odell to return to the col that night, as he and Irvine intended to do. So, Odell descended late in the afternoon, continually looking back in the hope of spotting something. The evening was clear, and a bright moon came up later. Odell and John de Vars Hazard, another team member, maintained a vigil until late, but they saw no lights on the mountain, no flashlights. Nothing.

By morning, when it was clear that no one had returned to the upper camps—both visible from the col—a sick feeling of dread built in Odell. By noon, he could bear the suspense no longer and set off once more up the mountain. He spent a cold, blustery night at Camp 5 and continued to the top camp the following day, having sent back his two porters.

Cinematographer John Noel (right) waited in vain for a glimpse of Mallory and Irvine on their summit day. Before Odell began searching for the missing men a code (below) was worked out for signaling messages on the mountain by using blankets on the snow. Noel filmed the signal from the North Col (far right) saying Mallory and Irvine were given up for dead.

The tent was still shut up as he had left it. No one had been back.

Once more he wandered above, hoping for signs of the missing men. But he soon realized that among the broken rocks of that vast mountainside, he might search diligently for weeks and find nothing. From a height he estimated as 28,000 feet, he came miserably back to the tent and pulled out the sleeping bags.

Dragging them to a patch of snow above camp, he took advantage of a lull in the wind to lay them out in the form of a T. This was a pre-arranged signal for Hazard, down on the col, telling him, "No trace can be found; given up hope." Later that evening, Odell and Hazard would relay the sad message from the col to Advance Base Camp with more bags laid out in a cross.

From the top camp, Odell had retrieved Mallory's compass and an oxygen set modified to Irvine's design. On the morning of June 11 he and Hazard packed up what they could from the col, left the tents standing, and descended by the quickest route to Camp 3. Norton sent a coded message home to advise of the tragedy and began composing a dispatch for the newspapers.

"We were a sad little party," he wrote later of the last days in Base Camp. "…The tragedy was very near; our friends' vacant tents and vacant places at table were a constant reminder to us of what the atmosphere of the camp would have been had things gone differently."

Ruth Mallory learned the news two days before the story broke in the world's newspapers. She faced lonely widowhood with great courage. It was not difficult, she said, to believe that George's spirit was ready for another life, and his way of going to it was very beautiful. What grieved her almost beyond enduring was that their three small children would never know their father. "Oh Geoffrey," she wrote to Mallory's dearest friend, "if only it hadn't happened! It so easily might not have."

# Afterword

**M**ANY OF THOSE WHO KNEW MALLORY were convinced that he and Irvine must have climbed to the top of Mount Everest before they died. They could not picture someone of such drive giving up once his goal was in sight. Still, the matter couldn't be proved, and the honor of first ascent went to Edmund Hillary and Tenzing Norgay when they reached the summit in spring 1953 and descended safely.

We'll never know exactly what happened on June 8, 1924. An ice ax, later identified as belonging to Andrew Irvine, was found in 1933 on easy-angled slabs some 250 yards east of the first step. Unlikely as it seemed, on such innocent-looking ground, this was taken as evidence that an accident to one or both climbers occurred at this spot. No further clues emerged until 1975 when a Chinese mountaineer, Wang Hung-bao, told comrades that he had discovered an "English dead" lying at 27,000 feet on Everest. It has never been possible to question Wang in more detail, as he was killed the day after sharing that information. But from what he said, it appeared the body lay below and in a direct line with Irvine's iceax, and so it was widely assumed to be that of the younger man rather than George Mallory.

Throughout the 1990s a German researcher, Jochen Hemmleb, made a detailed study of documents and photographs of Everest's North Face in an effort to pinpoint exactly where Wang found the dead climber. Finding these remains was the main objective of the expedition in 1999. Conrad Anker, a member of the team who was searching the

George Mallory at the age of 20. "From boybood he belonged to the mountains," his friend Geoffrey Young wrote when George died, "as flame belongs to fire. He lived their romance, their simplicity, their open power, their unchanging loveliness. As a mountaineer he was a genius."

outer limits of Hemmleb's designated area, came upon the remains of George Mallory. This amazing discovery, 75 years after the loss of the Everest pioneer, tells us a lot about Mallory's preparations for that last climb. But it gives no indication of how high he reached. No camera was found which could have shown the route the two men took. No wonderful summit photograph. There was a broken rope around Mallory's waist, telling us they were tied together when one slipped. Irvine must also lie somewhere on the North Face; and perhaps it was him Wang Hung-bao found in 1975. We cannot be certain until a second body is found, but we can be sure the search will go on.

If, by some miracle, a camera turns up, undamaged, containing exposed film, it is possible it will yield precious images, even after so long. Then we may learn if Mallory and Irvine reached the world's pinnacle 29 years ahead of Hillary and Tenzing, but it won't show us what caused their fatal plunge.

The 1924 expedition members built a memorial (right) in honor of the 12 dead of the first three Everest expeditions. If Mallory's Vestpocket Camera, similar to the one above, were found, could it yield images that would solve the mystery of whether he and Irvine reached the top?

Probably we'll never find out what these two gallant men achieved on their last day. In a sense, it should not matter. They challenged the unknown and died in pursuit of an ideal. That they climbed so high in those early days of Himalayan mountaineering is remarkable enough, when clothing and equipment fell far short of today's standards, and little was known of the risks of high altitude. Their friend Howard Somervell was adamant that they had not died in vain. "The loss of these splendid men," he said, "is part of the price that has been paid to keep alive the spirit of adventure. Without this spirit life would be a poor thing, and progress impossible."

# Chronology

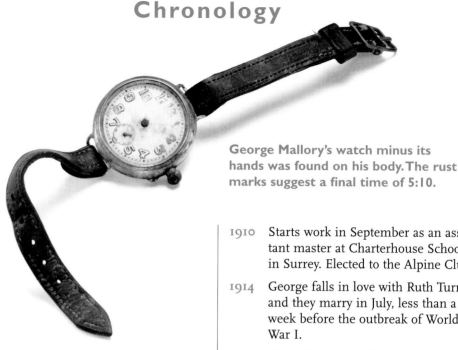

George Mallory's watch minus its hands was found on his body. The rust marks suggest a final time of 5:10.

1886   George Leigh Mallory born at Mobberley in Cheshire, England, on June 18, the second child of Reverend Herbert Leigh and Anne Beridge Mallory.

1896   Leaves home for Glengorse Preparatory School in Sussex, where he boards.

1900   Enters Winchester College, where he makes a reputation for himself as a gymnast and an athlete.

1904   At the age of 18 he gets his first taste of mountaineering when taken to the Alps by his housemaster. They climb several peaks, and Mallory is completely captivated.

1905   The "Ice Club" is founded at Winchester, and Mallory spends another season in the Alps before going up to Magdalene College, Cambridge, to study history.

1909   Meets the gifted mountaineer Geoffrey Winthrop Young, who becomes his lifelong friend. That summer they make the first ascent of the Alps' Nesthorn's southeast ridge.

1910   Starts work in September as an assitant master at Charterhouse School in Surrey. Elected to the Alpine Club.

1914   George falls in love with Ruth Turner, and they marry in July, less than a week before the outbreak of World War I.

1915   Clare, the first child of George and Ruth, is born on September 19.

1916   George is invalided home in May for treatment on an old ankle injury, and does not get back to France until October 1918. His daughter Beridge is born in September 1917.

1918   The War ends in November, but George is not demobilized until 1919.

1920   He arrives home from the Alps on August 21 as his son John is born.

1921   Resigns his teaching post and joins the Everest reconaissance expedition. Climbs to the North Col at 23,000 feet.

1922   With Norton and Somervell, Mallory reaches 26,985 feet, but this altitude record is broken a few days later by Finch and Bruce, climbing with oxygen, who attain 27,235 feet. In a third attempt 7 porters are killed in an avalanche.

1924   George Mallory and Sandy Irvine disappear high on Everest on June 10. They have taken oxygen and were spotted going strong, but no one knows if they made it to the top.

1999   George Mallory's body is found on Mount Everest.

# Resource Guide

Quotes from George Mallory are taken from his writings.

## BOOKS

Anker, Conrad and David Roberts. *The Lost Explorer.* New York: Simon & Schuster, 1999.

Breashears, David and Audrey Salkeld. *Last Climb, the Legendary Everest Expeditions of George Mallory.* Washington: National Geographic, 1999.

Bruce, C.G. and others. *The Assault on Mount Everest 1922.* London: Edward Arnold/ New York: Longmans, 1923.

Carr, Herbert (ed.). *The Irvine Diaries: Andrew Irvine and the Enigma of Everest 1924.* Reading: Gastons-West Col, 1979.

Finch, George Ingle. *The Making of a Mountaineer.* Bristol, Arrowsmith, 1924, enlarged 1988.

Hemmleb, Jochen with Larry A. Johnson and Eric Simonson. *Ghosts of Everest, The Search for Mallory and Irvine.* Seattle: The Mountaineers/London: Macmillan, 1999.

Holzel, Tom and Audrey Salkeld. *The Mystery of Mallory and Irvine.* London: Cape, 1986, 1996, 1999.

Howard-Bury, C.K. and others. *Mount Everest, The Reconnaissance 1921.* London:Arnold/New York: Longmans, 1922.

Norton, Lt. Col. E.F. and others. *The Fight for Everest 1924.* London: Arnold/New York: Longmans, 1925

Unsworth, Walt. *Everest.* Seattle: The Mountaineers (revised edition), 1999.

## MAGAZINE ARTICLES

Anker, Conrad. "Mystery on Everest." NATIONAL GEOGRAPHIC magazine, October 1999

Burrough, Bryan. "The Riddle of Everest." *Vanity Fair,* September 1999 and *GQ Australia,* December 1999/January 2000.

Hemmleb, Jochen and Larry Johnson. "Discovery on Everest." *Climbing,* September 1999.

Roberts, David. "Out of Thin Air." *National Geographic Adventure,* Fall 1999

## VIDEOS

"The Mystery of Mallory and Irvine," 1986 film, available from Nova, Public Broadcasting Service, 1999.

"Lost on Everest," Nova, Public Broadcasting Service, 2000.

"Lost on Everest," BBC, London, 1999.

## WEB SITES

www.everestnews.com

www.mountainzone.com/everest

www.pbs.org/wgbh/nova/everest

## PICTURE CREDITS

Cover (left), Royal Geographical Society; cover (right), Clare Millikan, Salkeld Collection; back cover, John Noel Photographic Collection; 2-3, The Alpine Club, photo by Geoffrey Young; 5, John Noel Photographic Collection; 7, Thomas Pollard; 9, Mrs. Molly Dalglish Collection, courtesy Peter Gillman; 10, Angela Gresham-Cooke Collection; 11, Mrs. Molly Dalglish Collection, courtesy Peter Gillman; 12, Angela Gresham-Cooke Collection; 13, National Portrait Gallery, London; 15 (upper), The Alpine Club, photo by Geoffrey Young; 15 (lower), Clare Millikan, Salkeld Collection; 17, Clare Millikan, Salkeld Collection; 18, Imperial War Museum; 20, Norton Everest Archive; 21, Royal Geographical Society; 23 (left), Clare Millikan; 23 (right), Royal Geographical Society, photo by George Mallory; 24-25, Royal Geographical Society, photo by George Mallory; 27, Royal Geographical Society, photo by Guy Bullock; 28-29, Royal Geographical Society, photo by Col. C.K. Howard-Bury; 29, Royal Geographical Society, photo by George Mallory; 31, T. Howard Somervell; 32, Royal Geographical Society, photo by John Noel; 32-33, The Alpine Club; 34, Royal Geographical Society, photo by T. Howard Somervell; 35, John Noel Photographic Collection; 37 (left), Ken Wilson Collection, photo by A.W. Wakefield; 37 (right), George Ingle Finch Collection; 38, Royal Geographical Society, photo by John Noel; 39, George Ingle Finch Collection; 40-41, Royal Geographical Society, photo by John Noel; 42, Salkeld Collection; 45, John Noel Photographic Collection; 46-47, John Noel Photographic Collection; 47, T. Howard Somervell; 48, Royal Geographical Society, photo by Bentley Beetham; 49, T. Howard Somervell; 50-51, T. Howard Somervell; 53 (upper), Royal Geographical Society, photo by N.E. Odell; 53 (lower), Mallory/Irvine Expedition/Jim Fagiolo/Liaison Agency; 54, The Sandy Irvine Trust, photo by Julie Steele; 55, Galen Rowell/Mountain Light; 56 (left), Keith Barclay; 56 (right), John Noel Photographic Collection; 57, John Noel Photographic Collection; 59, Clare Millikan; 60, National Geographic Photographer Mark Thiessen; 61, John Noel Photographic Collection; 62, Mallory/Irvine Expedition/Jim Fagiolo/Liaison Agency.

# Index

The world's largest nonprofit scientific and educational organization, the National Geographic Society was founded in 1888 "for the increase and diffusion of geographic knowledge." Since then it has supported scientific exploration and spread information to its more than nine million members worldwide.

The National Geographic Society educates and inspires millions every day through magazines, books, television programs, videos, maps and atlases, research grants, the National Geography Bee, teacher workshops, and innovative classroom materials.

The Society is supported through membership dues and income from the sale of its educational products. Members receive NATIONAL GEOGRAPHIC magazine—the Society's official journal—discounts on Society products, and other benefits.

For more information about the National Geographic Society and its educational programs and publications, please call 1-800-NGS-LINE (647-5463), or write to the following address:

National Geographic Society
1145 17th Street N.W.
Washington, D.C. 20036-4688
U.S.A.

Visit the Society's Web site:
www.nationalgeographic.com